Let's Build a Park!

by Kaye Gager   illustrated by Donald Wu

Scott Foresman
is an imprint of

Glenview, Illinois • Boston, Massachusetts • Chandler, Arizona
Upper Saddle River, New Jersey

Illustrations
Donald Wu

Photographs
Every effort has been made to secure permission and provide appropriate credit for photographic material. The publisher deeply regrets any omission and pledges to correct errors called to its attention in subsequent editions.

Unless otherwise acknowledged, all photographs are the property of Pearson Education, Inc.

8 ©Jamie And Judy Wild/Danita Delimont, Agent

ISBN 13: 978-0-328-50748-1
ISBN 10:   0-328-50748-2

10 V010 15 14 13

My friends and I had nothing to do.

We had no place to play.

Someone said, "Let's build a park!"

A park needs trees.

Dad planted them.

I helped dig the holes.

What other things do we need?

We still had no place to play.

Mom helped us build swings.

What other things do we need?

A park needs a garden.

We got some seeds.

Now it will be pretty!

An empty lot has become a park!

Some people stay all day.

I always go to the park after school.

Our new park has everything we need!

Gasworks Park

This building was once a power plant. When the plant closed down, the city of Seattle decided to build a park. People planted grass and built a picnic shelter. Some machines were turned into a playground. Now the old power plant is a place where everyone can have fun!

Gasworks Park was made from an old power plant.

Think and Share (Read Together)

1. Make a chart like the one below. List the things the friends did to make their park. List them in the right order.

Making a Park	
1	
2	
3	

2. Tell in your own words what this story is about.

3. Use the word *always* in a sentence that tells about your life.

4. Look at page 7. What other things could people do in the park?

Suggested levels for Guided Reading, DRA,™
Lexile,® and Reading Recovery™ are provided
in the Pearson Scott Foresman Leveling Guide.

Genre	Comprehension Skills and Strategy
Fiction	• Sequence • Author's Purpose • Summarize

Scott Foresman Reading Street 1.3.1

Scott Foresman
is an imprint of

ISBN-13: 978-0-328-50748-1
ISBN-10:   0-328-50748-2

9 780328 507481

90000>

We Make Soup!

By Leslie A. Rotsky

High-Frequency Words

I

have

the

has

Concept Words

carrots

potatoes

beans

tomatoes

onions

spoons

Word count: 24

Note: The total word count includes words in the running text and headings only. Numerals and words in chapter titles, captions, labels, diagrams, charts, graphs, sidebars, and extra features are not included.